A ROOKIE BIOGRAPHY

PHILLIS WHEATLEY

First African-American Poet

By Carol Greene

CHILDRENS PRESS®
CHICAGO

Phillis Wheatley (1753?-1784)

Library of Congress Cataloging-in-Publication Data

Greene, Carol.
   Phillis Wheatley : first African-American poet / by Carol Greene.
     p. cm. — (A Rookie biography)
   Includes index.
   ISBN 0-516-04269-6
   1. Wheatley, Phillis, 1753-1784—Biography—Juvenile literature.
2. Afro-American women poets—18th century—Biography—Juvenile
literature. 3. Women slaves—United States—Biography—Juvenile
literature. [1. Wheatley, Phillis 1753-1784. 2. Slaves, 3. Afro-Americans—
Biography. 4. Women—Biography.] I. Title. II. Series: Greene, Carol.
Rookie biography.
PS866.W5Z597   1995
811′.1—dc20
[B]   94-37516
                                             CIP
                                             AC

Phillis Wheatley
was a real person.
She lived from around
1753 until 1784.
Phillis was a slave
who wrote poems.
This is her story.

TABLE OF CONTENTS.

Chapter 1

The Journey

It was dark,
so dark,
and very, very hot.
Warm, sticky bodies pressed
against the little girl.
She could not move.

She tried to take
a deep breath,
but she could not
find any fresh air.
A thick, awful smell
filled the air.

People were crowded into the hold of
slave ships on the way to America.

The little girl was
on a slave ship sailing
from Africa to America.
She was locked
with other slaves
in the ship's hold
below the deck.

The slaves had
no light. They
had no toilets.
They sat or lay,
all crammed
together on the
hard wooden floor.

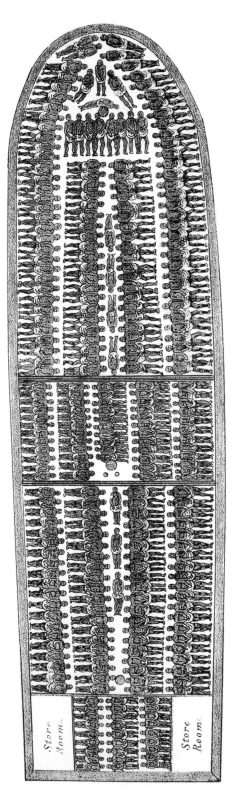

**This drawing shows how
slaves were sometimes
packed into a ship's hold.**

Twice each day, the slaves
were taken on deck
to do exercises.
They were fed only
rice and water.

The slave traders did not
want their slaves to die.
They could not sell
a dead slave.
But many died anyway and
were thrown into the sea.

Slaves who were too weak or sick to go on the ship were left to die on land.

The little girl could not
remember what happened
before she came to the ship.
Only one picture
of her old life
still lived in her mind.

That picture showed
the first morning sunbeam
shining on the land.
The little girl's mother
was bowing low
before that golden beam.

Now, in the awful darkness,
the little girl made herself
as small as she could
and watched her golden picture.

She may have come from
what is now Senegambia
in West Africa.
Maybe a chief from
another village set fire
to her village one night.
That often happened.

Slaves were taken from their villages and tied together
for the long march to the slave markets.

Then the chief caught people
as they ran from the fire.
He tied them together
and made them walk
to slave markets by the sea.

11

The slaves were sold to ship captains at slave markets
on the coast of Africa (top). The slaves were then taken
on ships to America, where they were sold again (bottom).

African slaves did most of the work on the big
farms in the southern American colonies.

Captains of slave ships
came to the markets
and bought the slaves.
Later, they sold them
at other slave markets
in America.

One day, the little girl
felt the ship stop.
Rough hands grabbed her
and washed her.
Then she was taken ashore
to see if anyone would buy her.

Although it was summer,
the little girl was cold.
She had no clothes,
just an old piece of rug
to wrap around herself.

So she stood shivering
and looking at the ground.
Then a woman stopped
in front of her
and said something.

The little girl could not
understand the words.
But the woman's voice was gentle.
The little girl raised her head.
Kind eyes looked at her.

Then the woman took her hand
and led her away.
Just once, the woman looked
back at the ship.
Its name was *Phillis*.

And so the woman called
the little girl Phillis, too.

The town of Boston (above) as it looked when Phillis lived there. The Old South Church (bottom left) and the Old State House (bottom right) were two of the larger buildings in Boston at that time.

Chapter 2

A New World

Phillis was eight years old
when she came to her new world,
so far away from Africa.
For a little while,
she was scared to death—
but just for a little while.

Soon Phillis began to learn.
The more she learned,
the more she wanted to learn.

She learned that she now
lived in Boston, in the
colony of Massachusetts.
Her owners were
John and Susannah Wheatley.

But they didn't treat Phillis
much like a slave.
They saw how quickly
she learned English and
how much she loved words.

So they let
their daughter,
Mary, teach
Phillis how to
read and write.
Most slaves
were not allowed
to learn these
things.

Some people did
not believe Phillis
could have written
the poems. So
John Wheatley
wrote this letter
telling how well
Phillis learned
English.

Phillis was brought from Africa to America in the Year 1761, between seven and eight years of Age. Without any assistance from School Education, and by only what she was taught in the Family, she, in sixteen Months Time from her Arrival, attained the English Language, to which she was an utter stranger before, to such a degree as to read any of the most difficult Parts of the Sacred Writings, to the astonishment of all who heard her.

As to her Writing, her own Curiosity, led her to it; and this she learnt in so short a Time, that in the year 1765, she wrote a letter to the Rev. Mr. Occum, the Indian Minister, while in England.

She has a great inclination to learn the Latin Tongue, and has made some progress in it.

This Relation is given by her Master, who bought her, and with whom she now lives.

John Wheatley (signed)

Mary used the Bible
and poems to teach Phillis.
Phillis soon loved them.

Phillis never had
healthy lungs.
Sometimes she got sick.
But she always went back to work
as soon as she could.

By the time Phillis was nine,
she could read the Bible
and understand it,
even the hard parts.

By the time she was 12,
she could read poems
and write them too.

By then, the Wheatleys knew
that Phillis was special.
They gave her a room of her own,
with a warm fire.
They gave her all the candles
she needed for light.

Phillis was at home
in her new world now,
and, most of the time,
it was a good world.

The State House (bottom) and
a windmill (below) at Newport,
Rhode Island, where the
Wheatleys took vacations.
Eunice Fitch (right) invited
Phillis to her home in Boston.

Chapter 3

The Poet

Mrs. Wheatley didn't want
Phillis to make friends
with other black people.
She wanted Phillis to
visit only white people.

But Phillis was black
and she was a slave.
She didn't feel comfortable
with white people.
So she often felt lonely.

The Wheatleys took vacations
in Newport, Rhode Island.
That is probably where
Phillis met Obour Tanner,
her one black woman friend.

"'Twas mercy brought me from my pagan land
Taught my benightened soul to understand
That there's a God, that there's a Savior too.
Once I redemption neither sought nor knew
Some view our sable race with scornful eye:
"Their color is a diabolic dye."
Remember, Christians, Negros, black as Cain,
May be refined and join the angelic train."

Phillis wrote this poem the night after she met Obour Tanner.

Obour was a slave too.
She and Phillis wrote
letters to one another.

Phillis also became
a strong Christian.
Her faith in God was
very important to her.

George Whitefield
(1714-1770) was a
famous minister
in England and
America.

Once she heard a minister
named George Whitefield preach.
He believed that *all* people
were equal in God's sight.

When Whitefield died,
Phillis wrote a poem about him.
One line said:
　"We hear no more the music
　　of thy tongue . . ."

People loved that poem.
By now, Phillis was one of
the best poets in America.
And she was only 17.

Mrs. Wheatley put some
of Phillis's poems together.
They were published as
a book in England.

P O E M S

O N

VARIOUS SUBJECTS,

RELIGIOUS AND MORAL.

BY

PHILLIS WHEATLEY,

NEGRO SERVANT to Mr. JOHN WHEATLEY,
of BOSTON, in NEW ENGLAND.

L O N D O N:
Printed for A. BELL, Bookseller, Aldgate; and sold by
Messrs. COX and BERRY, King-Street, *BOSTON.*

MDCCLXXIII.

A book of Phillis's poems was published in England in 1773.

Soon people in England wanted
to know more about Phillis.
Mrs. Wheatley's son was
traveling there anyway.
So Mrs. Wheatley sent
Phillis with him.

In England, Phillis went
to many parties.
She met important people.
She wrote to Obour that
everyone's kindness to her
"fills me with astonishment."

London in the late 1700s. While Phillis was there, she met Benjamin Franklin (below), the famous American.

Some of Phillis's new friends wanted her to meet the king of England.

Dearest Phillis:

It pains me to write such news, but both Father and Master John agree I must before it is too late. Mother was taken ill shortly after you left and has grown steadily worse. She can no longer rise out of bed, and I fear she may not live to see the baby. She is well taken care of, but pines endlessly for you. Each day she looks at your picture and murmurs, "My Phillis," and says to friends, "This is my youngest daughter, Phillis."

I know your health has improved there, but I cannot bear the thought of Mother never seeing you again. If you could find it in your heart to return home, we all agree it might give her the will to fight this illness.

I cannot tell you what to do. It will have to be your own decision. Please believe that both John and I pray it will be the right one for both you and Mother. God bless you.

Mary

Mary Wheatley wrote this letter to Phillis in England, asking her to come back to Boston.

But that never happened.
Word came that
Mrs. Wheatley was ill.
Phillis hurried home
to be with her.

Chapter 4

Free

During the next few years,
three important things
happened to Phillis.

First, the Wheatleys set her free.
She still lived with them.
But she wasn't a slave.

Second, Mrs. Wheatley died.
Phillis missed her terribly.
"I was treated by her
more like her child
than her servant,"
she wrote to Obour.

The third event
changed life for everyone
in America.

The colonies wanted to
be free from England.
But they had to fight
a war to win their freedom.
The American Revolution
began in 1775.

Many events that led to the American Revolution took place
in Boston. In 1775, Paul Revere made a famous ride (above)
to warn the colonists that the British were coming. The
drawing below shows British troops landing in Boston harbor.

Much of the fighting
took place around Boston.
So Phillis saw and
heard many things.

People watching the Battle of Bunker Hill from a Boston rooftop.
This was one of the first battles of the American Revolution.

General George Washington led the American
Continental Army during the Revolutionary War.

She heard about
George Washington, leader
of the Continental Army.
He was a great man,
thought Phillis.
She wrote a poem about him.

October 25, 1775

Sir.

I have taken the freedom to address your Excellency in the enclosed poem and entreat your acceptance, although I am not insensible of its inaccuracies.

Your being appointed by the Grand Continental Congress to be Generalissimo of the Armies of North America together with the fame of your virtues excites sensations not easy to suppress. Your generosities, therefore, I presume will pardon the attempt. Wishing your Excellency all possible success in the great cause you are so generously engaged in, I am

Your Excellency's Most Obedient Humble Servant

Phillis Wheatley

Phillis sent this letter with the poem she wrote to George Washington.

In her poem, Phillis
used fine, fancy words
the way poets did then.
"Proceed, great chief, with
virtue on thy side . . ."

George Washington's reply to Phillis's letter, and Washington's headquarters in Cambridge.

Washington liked the poem.
He asked Phillis to visit him.
So she went to his headquarters
in Cambridge, Massachusetts.

There the busy general
talked with Phillis
for half an hour.
No one knows what they said.

But that meeting was
an important moment
in Phillis Wheatley's life.

Chapter 5

Sad Years

The last years of Phillis's
short life were hard.
No one had much money
in a country at war.
As time went by,
all the Wheatleys died.

Phillis had to take
care of herself.
But how could she?
She couldn't get
a job writing poems.

Then Phillis married
a free black man
named John Peters.
At first they did well
and lived in a fine house.
Then times got hard again.

John Peters began
to have money problems.
He ended up in jail.

Phillis was often sick during the last years of her life.

Phillis had three babies.
But they all died.
Phillis's own health
grew worse and worse.

. . . I, young in life, by seeming cruel fate
Was snatch'd from *Afric's* fancy'd happy seat;
What pangs excrutiating must molest,
What sorrows labour in my parent's breast?
Steel'd was that soul and by no misery mov'd
That from a father seiz'd his babe belov'd. . . . .

Last Lord's Day, died Mrs. Phillis Peters (formerly Phillis Wheatley), aged thirty-one, known to the world by her celebrated miscellaneous poems. Her funeral is to be this afternoon, at four o'clock, from the house lately improved by Mr. Todd, nearly opposite Dr. Bullfinch's at West Boston, where her friends and acquaintances are desired to attend.

The announcement of Phillis's death appeared in a Boston newspaper.

Phillis Wheatley spent
her last days in a
house for poor people.
She died on December 5, 1784.

Phillis was 31 when she died.
She couldn't know that
over 200 years later,
people would remember her
and call her "the mother of
black literature in America."

Important Dates

1753   (year uncertain)—Born, probably in Senegambia, West Africa, to parents whose names are not known

1761   Captured by slave traders
Bought by Susannah Wheatley in Boston, Massachusetts

1770   Wrote first major poem, to George Whitefield

1773   Visited England
Poems on Various Subjects, Religious and Moral published in London

1775   Wrote poem to George Washington

1776   Met with George Washington

1778   Married John Peters

1784   December 5—Died in Boston, Massachusetts

INDEX

Page numbers in boldface type indicate illustrations.

PHOTO CREDITS

The Bettmann Archive—2, 6, 7, 12 (top), 25, 29 (bottom), 33 (bottom), 37, 40

H. Armstrong Roberts—13, 16 (top), 35

Library of Congress—22 (top right), 27

North Wind Picture Archives—8, 11, 12 (bottom), 16 (bottom left & right), 33 (top), 34

Stock Montage—22 (bottom), 29 (top)

Illustrations by Steven Gaston Dobson—Cover, 4, 15, 21, 38, 43, 44, 45

TEXT EXCERPTS ACKNOWLEDGMENTS

Phillis Wheatley by Marilyn Jensen, © 1987 Lion Books, 210 Nelson Road, Scarsdale, NY 10583—pp. 52-53 for use on p. 18, p. 62 for use on p. 24, p. 119 for use on p. 30, p. 155 for use on p. 36, p. 158 for use on p. 37, epilogue for use on p. 45

To the Right Honourable the Earl of Dartmouth for granting permission to reprint a Phillis Wheatley poem excerpt to the Earl as reprinted in *Phillis Wheatley and Her Writings* by William H. Robinson, © 1984 Garland Publishing, Inc., New York & London—p. 122 for use on p. 44

ABOUT THE AUTHOR

Carol Greene has degrees in English literature and musicology. She has worked in international exchange programs, as an editor, and as a teacher of writing. She now lives in Webster Groves, Missouri, and writes full-time. She has published more than 100 books, including those in the Childrens Press Rookie Biographies series.

ABOUT THE ILLUSTRATOR

Of Cajun origins, Steven Gaston Dobson was born and raised in New Orleans, Louisiana. He attended art school in the city and worked as a newspaper artist on the *New Orleans Item*. After serving in the Air Force during World War II, he attended the Chicago Academy of Fine Arts in Chicago, Illinois. Before switching to commercial illustration, Mr. Dobson won the Grand Prix in portrait painting from the Palette and Chisel Club. In addition to his commercial work, Steven taught illustration at the Chicago Academy of Fine Arts and night school classes at LaGrange High School. In 1987, he moved to Englewood, Florida, where he says "I am doing something that I have wanted to do all of my 'art life,' painting interesting and historic people."